Forgotten Patriot

The Story of HAYM SALOMON

by DAVID ALLEN LEWIS

ISRAEL and the USA | RESTORING THE LOST PAGES OF AMERICAN HISTORY

Published by
Bridges for Peace International
P.O. Box 1093
Jerusalem, Israel

Printed in the United States of America
ISBN: 965-7155-25-8

All sums of money are in US dollars, unless otherwise noted.

Visit our Web site
www.bridgesforpeace.com

Foreword

I am filled with a great deal of personal satisfaction that Bridges for Peace is publishing this booklet by my father, Dr. David Allen Lewis.

I have one of those larger-than-life type fathers, who had a tremendous impact not only on his children but also on the world at large through his ministry in the United States and around the world. He was the pastor of two churches early in his ministry, but the bulk of his ministry was spent as a traveling evangelist. As a family, we traveled throughout the United States, Canada, and other countries.

"The Bible says…" peppered many of his sermons. Growing up, I knew that the Bible was our principal authority in life. My father's sermons were never boring. He specialized in Bible prophecy for today. He was fascinated with Israel, eventually traveling there 67 times. After services, my father would be surrounded by people asking questions. They soaked up his knowledge and wisdom like a sponge. People often remarked to me, "It must be wonderful to live with such a man."

He had a deep love for the nation and people of Israel, and God blessed him with many divine appointments. He would sit at a coffee shop in Jerusalem, and almost invariably someone fascinating would sit next to him. Many lasting relationships with Israelis occurred in just this way. He was privileged to meet with Prime Minister Menachem Begin 19 times over the years. Their meetings were not just photo ops, but often deeply moving times when the prime minister and my father would sit and discuss the prophecies of Isaiah, Jeremiah, Ezekiel, and other prophets.

This booklet will give you an idea of the love and respect my father feels for the Jewish people. It is my hope that as you read it, you will realize just how much a blessing Haym Salomon was to the United States, and that you will be stirred to learn about many other Jewish people who have brought great blessing to the world through their endeavors. In Genesis 12:3, the last phrase of this covenantal promise to Abraham says, "and in you all the families of the earth shall be blessed." The story of Haym Salomon is one way this Scripture has been fulfilled.

Rebecca J. Brimmer

Rebecca J. Brimmer
International President and CEO
Bridges for Peace

Dedicated to the memory of

G. DOUGLAS YOUNG

founder of Bridges for Peace,
with whom my wife and I enjoyed a close
relationship and highly respected

Haym Salomon

Table of Contents

HAYM SALOMON REVOLUTIONARY PATRIOT

The SPEAKER pro tempore. Under a previous order of the House, the gentleman from California (Mr. DANIELSON) is recognized for 10 minutes.

Mr. DANIELSON. Mr. Speaker, today is the first day of issue by the U.S. Postal Service of a commemorative stamp to honor Haym Salomon, a great patriot of the American Revolution. Enscribed "Haym Salomon—Financial Hero," the stamp is one of four issued as a series to honor "Contributions to the Cause" and to commemorate the initial role they played in our American Revolution.

The stamp further commemorates the Bicentennial program for Haym Salomon, which was conducted by the Los Angeles District Council of the Jewish War Veterans of the United States on Sunday, January 26, 1975. The fine work of that Council, its auxiliary, and its friends has resulted in this recognition of Haym Salomon's magnificent work in furtherance of the American Revolution.

Haym Salomon, merchant, banker, and Revolutionary War financier, was born in Poland of Jewish-Portuguese parents in 1740. An advocate of Polish independence, he fled to England in 1771 and then to America, where he opened a brokerage office in New York.

He was in New York only a few months before he joined the Sons of Liberty, a group of revolutionary patriots, and was twice arrested and imprisoned by the British. Later, in Philadelphia, Salomon became financial agent in America for the French Government and was one of the leading dealers in bills of exchange and other securities. As a large depositor in Robert Morris' Bank of North America, Salomon contributed to maintaining the new government's credit. When Morris was appointed Superintendent of Finance, he turned to Salomon for help in raising the money needed to carry on the war and later to have the emerging nation from financial collapse. Salomon advanced direct loans to the government and also gave generously of his own resources to pay the salaries of government officials and army officers. With frequent entries of "I sent for Haym Salomon," Morris' diary for the years 1781–84 records some 75 transactions between the two men.

After the war, Salomon was almost penniless and died in 1785 before he could rebuild his business. Salomon, Morris and George Washington are the subjects of Lorado Taft's "Great Triumvirate of Patriots" monument in Chicago.

As we approach our Nation's Bicentennial, it is most appropriate that we pause to pay our respect to those who made freedom in America possible. We are greatly indebted to the band of American revolutionaries who broke the bonds of oppression and tyranny and secured the fortune of freedom to our people. It was an act of total dedication when the Signers of the Declaration of Independence, on July 4, 1776, adopted Thomas Jefferson's immortal words:

And for the support of this Declaration, with a firm Reliance on the Protection of divine Providence, we mutually pledge to each other our Lives, our Fortunes, and our sacred Honor.

This mutual pledge of dedication marked the dawn of free government for people in America and throughout the world. The thousands of patriots who joined the Signers also pledged their lives, their fortunes and their sacred honor. The great patriot whom we honor today, Haym Salomon, is one of these, for as he too accepted this pledge, he also carried the lead to insure the funds essential to the success of our American Revolution. He, too, pledged his life, his fortune, and his sacred honor.

United States Postal Service, 1975   Printing on the glue side

CHAPTER ONE

The Forgotten Patriot

*"This Ezra came up from Babylon; and
he was a skilled scribe in the Law of Moses,
which the LORD God of Israel had given.
The king granted him all his request,
according to the hand of the LORD his
God upon him...And I, even I, Artaxerxes
the king, issue a decree to all the treasurers
who are in the region beyond the River,
that whatever Ezra the priest, the scribe of
the Law of the God of heaven, may require
of you, let it be done diligently."*

EZRA 7:6, 21

istory has almost forgotten one of the most important figures in the saga of America. That person was Haym Salomon, a Jew of Philadelphia, a patriot who played a crucial role in the American Revolution. Who was Haym Salomon, and why has he been all but forgotten?

In 1975, the United States Postal Department published a stamp that had an unusual feature—it was printed on both sides. My extensive inquiries indicate that this series of stamps are the only stamps in philatelist history that were printed on the glue side! Salomon was honored in one of a series of bicentennial commemorative stamps. On the glue side of the stamp, in pale green ink, were printed these words: "Financial Hero—Businessman and broker Haym Salomon was responsible for raising most of the money needed to finance the American Revolution and later to save the new nation from collapse."

"Responsible for raising most of the money"...How those words gripped my attention! An overwhelming thought raced through my mind—if that is true, why did my history textbooks in grade school, high school, and college make no mention of this remarkable patriot? Could the postal department be printing a fantasy?

There is a large statue of Haym Salomon, George Washington, and Robert Morris in a traffic circle in downtown Chicago. Motorists pass by, unheeding, hardly wondering who stands beside the likeness of the father of our country. Some curious pedestrian might ponder, "George Washington I know. I seem to vaguely recall Robert Morris, but Haym Salomon, who are you?"

Statue of Robert Morris, George Washington, and Haym Salomon in downtown Chicago

It took me over 10 years of research before I finally put the story together. Historical material is sparse, but enough records exist to make a strong case for the concept that without the efforts of Mr. Salomon there might not even be a United States of America today.

Salomon was the principal financier of the American Revolution. Without the money he gave and raised, we would no doubt have lost the war with England. That being the case, it is probable that today instead of the United States of America, there would be a number of small nations occupying our lands. Alaska would still belong to Russia. There would be a French nation, an English-speaking republic, a Spanish country, a German, a Scandinavian, and an Italian nation. In other words, North America would look like the divided states of Europe.

The fate of Canada would be anybody's guess. Europe would have lost the Second World War against Hitler and the Nazis. It is possible the whole world could be under a Nazi regime. The swastika would fly over the nations of North America. There is little doubt that without U.S. intervention the Germans would have won the Second World War. What if there had not been a U.S.A.? What if George Washington had lost the war for lack of finance? Charles Hart is not wrong to write, "...without Haym Salomon, this 'broker,' we might very much fear there would not be a United States of America as we are privileged to know it."[1]

Salomon sometimes said that America was the promised land for the Jews—for now. But he dreamed of a day when Jerusalem would rise from the dust, when the Jews would return to their ancient homeland and build their glorious temple anew. Little did he realize what the future would hold. Could he have possibly dreamed that America would be an instrument in the hands of God to bless Israel in a latter day?

Salomon was not the only Jew to support the Revolution. Money in the Jewish community actively participated in a number of ways:

> At the outbreak of the Revolution, the Jews numbered two thousand of a total population of two million, or one-tenth of one per cent. Some of these Jewish settlers had developed extensive interests in the principal seaport towns of Newport, Philadelphia, New York, Charleston, and Savannah. They were chiefly engaged in inter-colonial and English Trade.

Some of the Jewish Traders of Newport and Philadelphia were among the largest ship owners in America. Their business interests, therefore, were on the side of England. To support the Revolution meant certain economic ruin. Nevertheless, the Jews were, almost to a man, supporters of the cause of Separation. Jewish names figure conspicuously in various Non-Importation Agreements and other measures designed to frustrate British trade. Members of the Jewish community were among the first to volunteer when war with England broke out. The Jews were found in contingents from nearly all the colonies, and their records as soldiers were brilliant...It is significant that the first American President, George Washington, took occasion to voice his regard and good will toward the Jewish people in several letters addressed to various Jewish communities in the United States.[2]

Many Jews fought as soldiers in George Washington's Revolutionary Army, and many contributed financially to the cause, but none did as much as Haym Salomon, one of the great heroes of American history—a forgotten hero, the wandering Jew from Poland.

The French armies came to the aid of the American revolutionaries and were a very important factor in the war effort. Here too, Salomon played a key role. "As the French troops began to pour in, he handled all the funds for the support and maintenance of their sea and land forces. 150,000,000 livres [old French monetary unit], on which he received the regular mercantile commission. All the money he made through these transactions, he invested in the Revolutionary cause."[3]

Salomon was early America's most successful broker. He bought and sold financial papers and instruments to raise money for Robert Morris, Superintendent of Finance for the Continental Congress. The Continental Congress had no power to raise taxes, and the war effort was continually on the brink of disaster. Without Salomon, the war would have been lost. After the war was over, the new nation was bankrupt. Once again Haym Salomon came to the financial aid of the U.S.A., rescuing our fledgling nation from bankruptcy and virtual extinction.

It can be documented that Salomon gave his personal fortune and, in addition, raised huge sums of money through business transactions, buying financial papers and leverage accounts on various European and American markets. He could have made himself rich and left a fine estate for his lovely wife and children. Instead, he died sick and penniless at the age of 45 on January 6, 1785. He had given all he had, and now his body lies in a lonely, unmarked, forgotten grave in Philadelphia. Why has his memory become so faded in the pages of American history?

It is not altogether a matter of Gentile anti-Semitism that Salomon's memory is lost to us. Salomon immigrated to Colonial America from Poland. The Jewish community of Philadelphia was mostly German. The German Jews did not want this Polish Jew to get so much credit, and they tried to minimize the contribution Salomon had made to the war effort. This is one of the strangest ironies in the chronicles of our nation.

When a proposal was made to erect a suitable monument to the memory of Haym Salomon, "Max J. Kohler, of German Jewish descent and an able student of American history, was among those who opposed the monument. The project to honor Salomon, he maintained, was motivated not so much by the wish to enshrine the memory of the man, as by the desire of the Polish Jewish federation to emphasize the fact that Polish Jews had come to these shores long before the Russian pogroms of 1881. The sharp differences between Kohler and his cohorts on one side and the 'Polish' Salomonians on the other side were to some degree a reflection of the rivalry between the old-line German Jewish settlers and the newer, aspiring East European element in American Jewish life."[4]

To this day, revisionist historians still try to deny Salomon his rightful place in history, but enough of the records exist to assure that any honest scholar who pursues the truth about America's Jewish patriot will find the evidence, and more. Our purpose in writing this book is to help restore Haym Salomon's rightful place in history.

This is the story of the forgotten patriot, a wandering Jew.

פִּתְחוּ
שְׁעָרֵי
צֶדֶ־ק

פִּתְחוּ
שְׁעָרִים
וְיָבוֹא
גּוֹי־צַ־ק

Artistic and idealistic depiction of Jews arriving in early America

CHAPTER TWO

The Wandering Jew

"You yourselves write a decree concerning the Jews, as you please, in the king's name, and seal it with the king's signet ring; for whatever is written in the king's name and sealed with the king's signet ring no one can revoke. So the king's scribes were called...And he wrote in the name of King Ahasuerus, sealed it with the king's signet ring, and sent letters by couriers on horseback, riding on royal horses bred from swift steeds. By these letters the king permitted the Jews who were in every city to gather together and protect their lives...A copy of the document was to be issued as a decree in every province and published for all people, so that the Jews would be ready...The Jews had light and gladness, joy and honor."

ESTHER 8:8–11, 13, 16

aym Salomon, son of Rabbi Salomon, was born at Lissa, Poland in 1740. He had little formal education, but taught himself to speak English and French and could make himself understood in several other languages. "In his wanderings, he acquired a working knowledge of German, French, Italian, Russian, Polish, English, and perhaps some other tongues. Far more to the point, he did acquire an unusual knowledge of finance and made friends among the bankers of the most important European commercial centers."[5]

He left Poland, spent some time in Europe, and finally arrived in America some time before 1772. After his arrival in New York, Salomon established a successful brokerage business. In New York, he found abeautiful bride. At the age of 37, he took the lovely 15-year-old Rachel Franks to be his wife. Soon they had a son whom they named Ezekiel. Haym and Rachel were deeply in love, and he was able to support her in comfort for a while, but then tragedy struck. Haym was put into a British jail. Most of the small fortune he had amassed in a short time was lost.

Salomon had gotten involved with the American patriots and the cause of the Revolution. This led to his imprisonment at the hands of the British, who had captured New York City. He was sentenced to be executed. Salomon paid a large bribe in gold coins to his Hessian guard and escaped. From New York, he made his way to Philadelphia, the seat of the American government and the second largest city in the entire British Empire. Salomon had gotten very sick in the British prison, and the journey was tiring and fraught with dangers on every hand. After arriving in Philadelphia, he was graciously taken in and cared for by families of the Jewish community. There in the seat of the Continental United States government, Salomon became ever more dedicated to the cause of the Revolution. Shortly, he was joined by his wife and child.

Once settled in Philadelphia, Salomon started doing brokerage business in a corner of a coffeehouse. This was not an uncommon practice for brokers. Coffeehouses served as meeting places, the crossroads for the men of the community. Salomon was deeply moved when he read a letter from James Thatcher, which appeared in a local newspaper: "Our poor soldiers are reduced to the very edge of famine, their patience is exhausted by complicated sufferings, and their spirit is almost broken."

The sorry condition of the American forces is described in the most bleak of terms in Washington Irving's *Life of George Washington*:

> The winter set in early, and was uncommonly rigorous. The transportation of supplies was obstructed; the magazines were exhausted; and the commissaries had neither money nor credit to enable them to replenish them. For weeks at a time, the army was on half allowance—sometimes without meat, sometimes without bread, sometimes without both. There was a scarcity, too, of clothing and blankets, so that the poor soldiers were starving with cold as well as hunger.
>
> Washington wrote to Governor Reed of Pennsylvania, entreating aid and supplies from that State to keep his army from disbanding. "We have never," said he, "experienced a like extremity at any period of the war."
>
> To suffer was the lot of the Revolutionary soldier.
>
> A rigorous winter had much to do with the actual distresses of the army, but the root of the evil lay in the derangement of the currency. Congress had commenced the war without adequate funds and without the power of imposing direct taxes. To meet pressing emergencies, it had emitted paper money, which for a time, passed currently at par; but sank in value as further emissions succeeded, and that already in circulation went unredeemed...thus the country gradually became flooded with a continental currency, as it was called; irredeemable, and of no intrinsic value...[6]

Onto the stage of history walks the wandering Jew from Poland, Haym Salomon, to make an unheralded contribution that no less than saved the day for George Washington and the American army.

Haym Salomon began to tour the army camps, to see what conditions the soldiers were living under. It was a bleak and discouraging picture that he found. Shirley Milgrim wrote: "When Salomon had recovered from his ordeal, he explored the camp with a young lieutenant. The Continental northern force was a sorry sight. No one owned a complete uniform, a new musket, or an unbent bayonet, it seemed. Lean men in buckskin shirts, coonskin caps, and shoes tied together with rope stood around idly outside their patched tents. Salomon had heard of the poverty of some members of the American force, but to actually see these conditions shook him up badly."[7]

Although supplies were available for Washington's pitiful army, they were unattainable. Colonials were selling to the British enemies for gold coin and refused to accept American paper currency, which was worthless. The morale of the army was extremely low. Since this was an all-volunteer, irregular army, desertions were common. Less than 30% of the citizens of the colonies were in favor of the war against the British. Few colonials had read the Declaration of Independence, and few cared who won the war. Many colonials were getting rich off the war, catering to either side for commercial benefit. This fell out, principally, to the advantage of the British, who had assembled the mightiest military machine of the era and were backed by the vast wealth of the far-flung British Empire.

Salomon's coffeehouse brokerage gained fame throughout the 13 states and with the Europeans. So sound were his judgments, so profitable his ventures that people came from everywhere to have him make investments for them. Salomon was eager to serve the Revolutionary War effort and attempted time and again to make contact with Robert Morris, the treasurer of the Continental Congress. He hoped to assist the government on a more direct and effective basis.

The story of Haym Salomon is succinctly told in the authoritative *Encyclopaedia Britannica*:

> SALOMON, HAYM—U.S. patriot who was a principal financier of the fledgling American republic and

a founder of the first Philadelphia synagogue, Mikvah Israel, for his Jewish co-religionists. In 1772, probably because of his revolutionary activities for Polish liberty, he fled to New York City, where he established himself as a commission merchant. He soon became a successful financier and supported the patriotic cause on the outbreak of the American Revolution. In 1776 the British, who controlled New York City, arrested Salomon: exposure suffered in prison soon led to his early death. He was paroled but was arrested again in 1778 on more serious charges; he escaped and went to Philadelphia. There he established a brokerage office and acted without salary as the financial agent of the French, doing all in his power to facilitate the Franco–American Alliance.

Among his many other contributions to the Colonies, Salomon subscribed heavily to government loans, endorsed notes, gave generously to soldiers, and equipped several military units with his own money. Robert Morris, the superintendent of finance from 1781 to 1784, appointed Salomon as broker to his office. Morris records in his diary that between 1781 and 1784 Salomon lent more than $200,000. In addition, he made private loans to prominent statesmen such as James Madison, Thomas Jefferson, and James Monroe, from whom he would not take interest. In all, the government owed Salomon more than $600,000. Generations of his descendants tried in vain to collect some portion of these loans, which had helped to impoverish Salomon in his last years.[8]

Salomon equipped many units of Washington's army with his own money and made private loans to prominent statesmen such as James Madison, James Monroe, and Thomas Jefferson.

From Jacob Marcus's account, we learn the following:

> Salomon was in the habit of lending money to some of the delegates of the continental Congress who were in desperate need, among them, James Madison. In August of 1782, the future president had written to Edmund Randolph: "I cannot in anyway make you more sensible of the importanceof your kind attention to the pecuniary remittances for me than by informing you that I have for some time past been a pensioner on the favor of Hyam Salomon, a Jew broker." The next month Madison was still in as bad shape as ever and reported that other members of the Congress were also in sore need of ready cash. He then borrowed some more money from Jacob I. Cohen, a Richmond merchant.
>
> But evidently even that was not sufficient, and so he directed his steps again to the office of Salomon. It is to be noted that this time Madison does not refer to him as a "Jew." "I am almost ashamed to reiterate my wants so incessantly to you," he wrote to Randolph again, "but they begin to be so urgent that it is impossible to suppress them. The kindness of our little friend in Front Street, near the coffee-house, is a fund which will preserve me from extremities, but I never resort to it without great mortification, as he obstinately rejects all recompense. The price of money is so usurious that he thinks it ought to be extorted from none but those who aim at profitable speculations. To a necessitous delegate, he gratuitously spares a supply out of his private stock.[9]

It is interesting to note that *Encyclopaedia Britannica* authenticates that the government owed Salomon more than $600,000. Other sources indicate that $800,000 can be documented. The real figure, if all the facts were known, is probably far higher. Taking the $800,000 figure and adding interest over 217 years, one arrives at a debt amounting to over $2.5 trillion owed to the heirs of Salomon!

The ketubah, marriage contract,
of Haym Salomon and Rachel Franks, New York, July 6, 1777

CHAPTER THREE

Rachel

*"Then Jacob kissed Rachel, and lifted up
his voice and wept...Rachel was beautiful
of form and appearance...Now Jacob loved
Rachel; so he said, 'I will serve you seven
years for Rachel your younger daughter.'"*

GENESIS 29:11, 17, 18

*"A voice was heard in Ramah, lamentation,
weeping, and great mourning, Rachel
weeping for her children, refusing to be
comforted, because they are no more."*

MATTHEW 2:18

achel Franks Salomon was the daughter of Moses B. Franks, a well-to-do New York merchant. She was married to Haym Salomon on July 6, 1777 on a lovely Sunday afternoon. The groom was 37 years old, the lovely bride a mere 15, but it seemed to be a marriage made in heaven. Never was Salomon any less than lovingly devoted to his beloved Rachel. She brought Salomon a dowry of 250 pounds. It was the custom of the time. Salomon, however, hardly needed it, as he was already prospering in his New York business.

When he was imprisoned by the British, triple tragedy struck. First, he was separated from Rachel and his son Ezekiel. Second, in prison he contracted tuberculosis, the dread disease that would end his life prematurely. Third, he lost his considerable wealth.

Salomon escaped the prison, fled to Philadelphia, leaving his family behind in New York, and arrived in the Quaker City a pauper, just a wandering Polish Jew. What Haym Salomon had in his mind and indomitable spirit, however, were treasures that the British could not take from him. He began to prosper in business and shortly became financially comfortable. It wasn't long until his family was able to join him in Philadelphia.

When the Salomons got established in Philadelphia, it was in grand style. Haym was able to purchase a fine house for his beloved Rachel, furnished with Chippendale and other fine furnishings. They were also able to employ a servant. Rachel shared Haym's sympathy for the Revolution, but nevertheless had some grave concerns for the future.

One thing dimmed Rachel's joy in life in Philadelphia, however. Her husband did not share his worries over money with her. His love was tender and protective. He wished, as a father might wish, that he could keep this precious child, Rachel, from worries forever. But gossip reached her ears that a good deal of the hundreds of thousands of dollars Haym had earned since he came to the Quaker City, he had insisted on lending to the Congress and its officials. Her best friends warned her that Haym seemed to care more for the War of Independence than he did for the security of his family—that he was sacrificing his health to impress Mr. Robert Morris.[10]

Even Haym's assistant began to resent the unreasonable demands on his employer. One day McRae revealed to Rachel that Congress had asked Haym to advance a whole year's pay to Mr. Jones, Mr. Randolph, and Mr. Madison of the Continental Congress. McRae was angry and told Rachel that their demands were just going too far. When Rachel asked McRae if Haym paid them what they asked, he replied testily that he not only paid what they requested, but upon noticing that Madison had been allotted 50 pounds less than the other two, he decided to give them all the same amount out of his own purse.

Rachel worried continually about Haym's health. His bouts of coughing gave her great concern. She was always urging him, along with the advice of his doctor, to get more rest. But he would tell her that he was not so old, and there would be plenty of time for rest when the war was over.

Milgrim weaves a conversation in her docu-history for us:

> Rachel summoned up the courage to ask, "Haym, if you stopped working, would we have enough money to live on? I mean, wouldn't it be better if I knew something about our situation? I really don't know what to think. I've never considered myself rich, and yet some people say we are quite wealthy."
>
> Salomon didn't answer.
>
> "And others say there are no savings."
>
> "They're both right," he replied.

"Ah, I see. We would be wealthy if it weren't for the loans. That's why there are no savings." She threw her arms around him. "You're just too good, too kind."

He looked annoyed. "The War of Independence is not a charity. It's an investment."

"But you know that you'll never get paid back."

He took her hand and kissed it. "Don't worry your pretty head. I saw a bolt of blue velvet on the dock today. I think I'll buy it for you, and you'll have a new dress. And if you will only stop worrying about my health, I'll bring you a fan and some French perfume."

"But Haym, our children—will there be something left for them to inherit from us?"

"Yes, a country where they'll be free to differ in the way they worship God and still enjoy the friendship of other people. I want most to leave the children an opportunity for happiness equal to that of the other citizens of a new nation and a feeling that they are as important a part of the new nation as anyone else."

Rachel couldn't argue with the man she respected and loved so much. She recognized the truth in what he said. Opportunity was a far more valuable legacy than dollars."[11]

Rachel bore four children to Haym Salomon, the fourth child being born just three months after his death. Rachel named the child Haym M. Salomon after his late father. Four children, all under the age of seven, and a young widow remained to mourn him. Because of his devotion to his adopted country, he left no financial legacy to his little family.

Rachel tried for months after Haym's death to collect on personal loans that he had made to Robert Morris, to Congress, and others. She was requested to turn all of her securities and certificates over to the state treasurer of Pennsylvania for evaluation. After several months, she made further inquiries and was informed that all of the papers relating to her inheritance had been "lost."

Finally Rachel was remarried to David Helbrun of New York City, who was able to adequately care for her and the children.

Haym Solomons,

BROKER to the Office of Finance, to the Conful General of France, and to the Treasurer of the French Army, at His Office in Front-Street, between Market and Arch streets, BUYS and SELLS on Commiſſion

BANK Stock, Bills of Ex-

change on France, Spain, Holland, and other parts of Europe, the W-ſt Indies,—and inland bills, at the uſual comm ſſion.——He Buys and Sells

Loan-Office Certificates, Con-

tinental and State Money, of this or any other State, Paymaſter and Quartermaſter General's Notes; theſe and every other kind of paper tranſactions (bills of exchange except c) he will charge his employers no more than ONE HALF PER CENT on his Commiſſion,

He procures Money on Loan

for a ſhort time, and gets Notes and Bills diſcounted.

Gentlemen and others, reſiding in this State, or any of the united States, by ſending their orders to this Office, may depend on having their buſineſs tranſacted with as much fidelity and expedition, as if they were themſelves preſent.

He receives Tobecco, Sugars, Tea, and every other ſort of Goods to Sell on Commiſſion; for which purpoſe he has provided proper Stores.

He flatters himself, his aſſidu-

ity, punctuality, and extenſive connections in his buſineſs, as a Broker, is well eſtabliſhed in various parts of Europe, and in the united ſtates in particular.

All perſons who ſhall pleaſe to favour him with their buſineſs, may depend upon his utmoſt exertion for their intereſt, and——

Part of the Money advanced, if required.

N. B. Paymaſter-General's Notes taken as Caſh for Bills of Exchange.

HORSES.

The Subſcriber has removed his

HORSES to a commodious ſtable in Church alley, where he has Opened a LIVERY. He provides

An advertisement for Haym Salomon's brokerage business

CHAPTER FOUR

Financing the Revolution

"And I appointed as treasurers over
the storehouse Shelemiah the priest and
Zadok the scribe, and of the Levites,
Pedaiah; and next to them was Hanan
the son of Zaccur, the son of Mattaniah;
for they were considered faithful, and their
task was to distribute to their brethren."

NEHEMIAH 13:13

obert Morris was born in Liverpool, England. In 1747, he immigrated to America and took an apprenticeship in the firm of Charles Willing, a merchant in Philadelphia. He showed great aptitude for the business and later became a partner in the firm.

Morris voted against the Declaration of Independence, but later became a signatory of the document. As a member of Congress, he worked continuously to raise money for munitions and supplies for the Revolutionary Army. He served as treasurer of the Continental Congress.

A curious relationship between Morris and the Polish Jew, Salomon, was to develop that would effect the destiny of this nation. One might wonder why Robert Morris, treasurer of the Continental Congress, delayed in contacting Haym Salomon for so long, when Salomon had indicated to him repeatedly in letters that he was able and willing to help the cause with finances.

That Robert Morris did not like Jews was an unmistakable fact. Indeed, the man was an anti-Semite. He only reluctantly, as a last resort, accepted help from Haym Salomon. He had been informed on several occasions of Salomon's willingness to help the American cause. Even Washington had written Morris, recommending that he contact Salomon. But Morris, in his prejudice, could only think of Jews as Shylocks and money grubbers, extorting excessive interest on each investment they made.

Morris made his first contact with Salomon on *Yom Kippur* (Day of Atonement), the holiest day on the Jewish calendar. Morris sent a messenger to find Salomon at the coffeehouse brokerage and was informed that he was at the synagogue for the high holy day service. Morris insisted, over his courier's vehement protest, that he go to the synagogue and get Haym Salomon out of the meeting to appeal for his help. On *Yom Kippur*, no Jew is even supposed to think about money. It would be blasphemous to touch money, write a check, or enter into any kind of financial transaction.

At the synagogue, Rabbi Gershom Mendes Seixas was conducting the early part of the service. A number of Jewish soldiers who had been with Washington at Valley Forge were present in the meeting, along with various visiting dignitaries.

Then, there was a knock at the door of the synagogue. What fool would knock on *Yom Kippur*? When the sexton opened the door, he was surprised by a Gentile asking for Haym Salomon. Salomon went outside to meet him and was handed an official-looking, sealed message. Breaking the seal, he found inside the envelope two bills of exchange and the following message:

> My Dear Mr. Salomon,
>
> The terrible emergency of the moment necessitates my turning to you at this hour. The office of finances has been unable to procure sufficient funds to cover the enclosed notes which must be discounted immediately. I have exhausted even my personal resources of aid. Since all else has failed, I must beg of you to act immediately with whatever resources you have to satisfy our distress.
>
> —Robert Morris

On *Yom Kippur*, a Jew empties his pockets of all material things and would not carry even the smallest coin, putting all thoughts of money out of his mind. It was on this holy day that Robert Morris, an insensitive man, chose to reach out to the Jew he despised.

Salomon was able to look beyond the disdainful arrogance of Morris. For he had a hope in his bosom that America would be a promised land for the Jews, where they could cease their wandering until the day that God would allow them to return to their own ancient homeland, rebuild Jerusalem and the Temple, and revive their nation. It was a burning dream in his heart and mind.

But this was *Yom Kippur*! Almost in a daze, he looked at the message again, noting its urgency. With a feeling of heaviness, he went to Rabbi Seixas to ask permission to speak to the congregation. When he began to exhort the men of the synagogue to go home and bring money for Washington's army, the place erupted in protest. Rabbi Seixas cried, "You blasphemer, you have already put inordinate demands on the Jews for your cause, now you defile our holiest day of atonement! Salomon, have you gone insane? How can you do this to us?"

Weeping, Salomon explained the need, saying, "Mr. Morris must have $20,000 for General Washington. He must have the money today. I will give the first $3,000."

Samuel Lyon spoke, "May God have mercy on me and forgive me. I will give $1,000."

Others called out pledges to be paid at day's end when *Yom Kippur* was over. The $20,000 was subscribed in 15 minutes. Robert Morris's messenger said to Salomon, "I have never in my life seen such a demonstration of patriotism, nor shall I ever see it again in my lifetime." He went back to Morris with the news that the money would be delivered after sundown. Even while being helped by Salomon, Morris spoke disparagingly of "the little Jew," and "the Jew broker." Only much later, did he grudgingly show respect for this most valued helper in the war effort.

"Judging from the fact that Mr. Salomon the broker is mentioned more than 100 times in the diary of the Superintendent of Finance, we may rest assured that Haym pitched in vigorously to help Morris."[12]

Salomon undertook to pay the salaries and living expenses of political leaders and officers of the Revolutionary Army out of his own monies. He was repaid very little of this investment, and only fragmentary records remain in the archives at the Library of Congress. But there is enough of a record to show what kind of a man he was.

> Haym Salomon not only helped keep the nation in finances through the sale of subsidies to France and Holland, he turned over to the United States all the commissions he thus earned. He also pledged his personal fortune to the Bank of North America, which would have otherwise closed, paid the salaries of James Madison and at least two other future Presidents of the United States, underwrote most of the expenses of Lafayette's Army...and neither he nor his heirs ever collected a dime of what was due him from the Government. He never even received a medal for his services!

How this came about is a most amazing story of unselfish service and of a government's ingratitude—a story without a known counterpart in any nation's history, and an example of utter lack of appreciation of what the Jewish race has meant to this and other countries.[13]

After writing to General George Washington indicating that he was willing to help the army by financing some of its officers, Salomon received a visit from Baron Frederick William von Steuben, a former officer of the Prussian army who volunteered to train Washington's troops. Von Steuben was destitute and embarrassed to have to call on Salomon. He told Salomon that his wages were only $3 a month, and when it was paid, it was in useless American paper money. The monthly salary of a private in the army, informed von Steuben, was only 20 cents. Von Steuben immediately received 1,000 pounds sterling from the Jewish broker. Subsequently, a stream of supplicants came to the "little Jew from Poland" to present their needs. No one with a legitimate need went away empty-handed.

Baron von Steuben

Because of his insight into world markets and finance, Salomon was able to raise the money to minister to most of these needs. He was the most highly sought after investment counselor and broker in America. Though his generosity eventually impoverished him, he enriched many investors through his uncanny skills. His signature on a document was the most desired approval in the world of finance of that era. Here is the text of one of the advertisements of his brokerage business (pictured on page 22):

HAYM SALOMON

Broker to The Office of Finance, To the Consul General of France and to the Treasurer of the French Army.

At his office in Front Street between Market and Arch Streets.

Buys and Sells on Commission, Bank Stock, Bills of Exchange on France, Spain, Holland and other parts of Europe, the West Indies and Inland Bills, at the usual Commissions. He buys and sells Loan Office Certificates, Continental and State Money of this or any other State, paymasters and quartermasters general notes; these and every other kind of paper transactions (bills of exchange excepted) he will charge his employers no more than one half of one per cent for his commission.

He procures Money on Loan for a short time and gives notes and bills discounted.

Gentlemen and others residing in this state or in any of the United States, by sending their orders to the office, may depend on having their business transacted with as much fidelity and expedition as if they were themselves present.

He receives tobacco, sugars, tea and every other sort of goods to sell on commission for which purpose he has provided proper stores.

He flatters himself that his assiduity, punctuality and extensive connections in his business as a broker is well established in various parts of Europe and in the United States in particular.

All persons who shall please to favor him with their business may depend upon his utmost exertion for their interest and part of the money advanced if desired.

Advertisements of this nature were posted as handbills and also printed in publications. Historian Albert Bushneff, Professor Emeritus of History, Harvard University, wrote of Salomon: "All Americans may acclaim Haym Salomon as a patriot, a benefactor to his Country, an inciter of patriotism to members of his race, to his countrymen, and to later generations. It looks as though his credit was better than that of the whole 13 United States of America."

Haym Salomon Jewish–American Hall of Fame Bronze Medal
Designed by Paul Vincze, 1973

CHAPTER FIVE

The Unpaid Debt

❦

*"Now all the people gathered together as one
man in the open square that was in front of the
Water Gate; and they told Ezra the scribe to
bring the Book of the Law of Moses, which the
LORD had commanded Israel. So Ezra the
scribe stood on a platform of wood which they
had made for the purpose; and beside him, at his
right hand, stood Mattithiah, Shema, Anaiah,
Urijah, Hilkiah, and Maaseiah; and at his left
hand Pedaiah, Mishael, Malchijah, Hashum,
Hashbadana, Zechariah, and Meshullam."*

NEHEMIAH 8:1, 4

*H*ow much is owed to this one man, Haym Salomon! The debt, which cannot even be measured in monetary value, will probably never be paid. Our nation should at least pay a token to the kinsmen of Haym Salomon, the Israelis. We could begin by determining that we shall no more yield to ungodly world pressures in regards to Israel, and by making it clearly known that we will stand by the nation of Israel.

The following quotation is found on a photocopy in our files. It is from page 914 of an encyclopedic reference work. We have lost any notations as to the identity of the source. It refers to Salomon as "most successful of the war brokers; he became, in effect, the Revolution's foremost banker after Morris. He succeeded at one point in negotiating a loan of $400,000 for General George Washington's army in 1779, and it is possible a sizable amount of the loan came from him personally. How much of *his own funds* he used to further the Revolution has never been determined and is still a matter of debate" (emphasis mine).

In the previous chapter, we cited the words of Charles Hart, that Salomon "also pledged his personal fortune to the Bank of North America, which would have otherwise closed." The importance of this is indicated by the following: "The financial needs of the colonies toward the end of the Revolution reached crisis proportions. To meet these needs, the Bank of North America was chartered in 1782. Because of doubts over the authority of Congress to charter a bank, it was incorporated in the state of Pennsylvania. This was the first private commercial bank in the United States as well as the first government-incorporated bank. Largely through the ability of Robert Morris, who headed the bank, foreign loans were secured and Washington's army [were] fed and clothed for the remainder of the war."[15]

Robert Morris is granted the credit on the pages of history, and he should be given his due, but Salomon also played a vital role in the saving of the Bank of America. Haym Salomon, the forgotten patriot! Charles Russell wrote:

> But one thing is clear. Haym Salomon produced for Morris a sum of money for those times immense and so again and again warded off inestimable disaster. We may be sure that not another man on the American side of the struggle could have set forth in cash such a sum or anything like it. Robert Morris of Willing, Morris and Stanwick—the foremost financial house in America—tried it and failed. The romance of business still remains unwritten in America. It has nothing more remarkable than this triumph of a Polish immigrant, nine years in the country, and the price he paid for it. The whole American Revolution seems now to the sober inquiring sense a thing incredible, but even that wild story has no chapter more startling.
>
> As an astute commentator aptly observes, the credit of Haym Salomon seemed greater than the credit of the entire United States. He produced the money; he delivered it...He was the regular reliance of the poor haunted Superintendent of Finance, relieving with timely advances a situation that had become more than threatening.
>
> He played the fairy godfather in the drama; he came in the nick of time to avert disaster. Men turned to him for financial wisdom as well as for financial support...Salomon deserves a golden page in the history of the United States, for his means and his services were at the disposal of the government.[16]

What a debt we owe! Think once more of George Washington's desperate plight. "So closed the year 1779. The colonies were not yet free...The national treasury was bankrupt. The patriots of the army were poorly fed and paid only with unkept promises."[17]

The third Continental Congress of the U.S.A. recognized the debt owed to Salomon's heirs, but never a penny was paid. As we note elsewhere in this book, *Encylopaedia*

Britannica figures the amount loaned by Salomon to the United States was at least $600,000.

Russell cites figures discussed in the 37th Congress, second session, which on July 2, 1862, through Senator Wilkinson, made a report declaring that the "claim is of undeniable merit." The compilation of original sums owing to the heirs of Haym Salomon amounted to $658,007.33, according to the 37th Congress. We are inclined to believe that this is far less than really was loaned by Salomon.[18]

Historian Jacob Marcus records that the sum of $800,000 owed to Salomon was fixed in the minds of many, although he comes short of actually documenting the amount. *Encyclopaedia Britannica* can be taken as excellent documentation that it was "more than $600,000."

Marcus tells the story of Salomon, who "was the real financial hero of the Revolution: 'the man that stood behind Morris and actually produced the actual sums with which the Revolution moved on.' He advanced to the government—in one form or another—about $800,000 of his own money, but when he died, leaving a young widow and helpless children, nothing was left for them."[19] We think, after extensive reading and research, that it may be demonstrated that at least $800,000 (and probably a lot more) was loaned to the colonies by Salomon.

Suppose the U.S.A. were to pay the debt today. Calculate the sum of $800,000 at 7% interest, compounded quarterly over a period of 217 years. The sum is astronomical due to the exponential factor of interest increase. We have had various mathematical and computer experts calculate the amount for us. It puzzles me that they come up with different amounts. The most conservative figure offered us is that the U.S.A. owes the heirs of Haym Salomon $2.5 trillion. The next time some congressman whimpers about aid to Israel, ponder these facts. Think of the unpaid debt we owe.

Salomon had a dream for the Jewish people, that America would be the place where they could find rest, and that one day this nation would be the instrument for reestablishing the national homeland of the Jewish people in Eretz Israel. In this day of rising anti-Semitism, I hope that dream will not be tarnished by Americans turning against Israel. As powerful efforts are being made to undermine support for Israel in the political arena, in the media, and even in the evangelical churches, we must redouble our commitment to the biblical mandate to be a comfort to Israel.

And to whom does the prophet Isaiah speak, *"Comfort, yes, comfort My people!" says your God. "Speak comfort to Jerusalem"* (Isaiah 40:1–2a)? It is not Israel that receives this command, but a later people of God, the Church.

To Zion, the Almighty exhorts: *"O Zion, you who bring good tidings, get up into the high mountain; O Jerusalem, you who bring good tidings, lift up your voice with strength, lift it up, be not afraid; say to the cities of Judah, 'Behold your God!'…But you, Israel, are My servant, Jacob whom I have chosen, the descendants of Abraham My friend"* (Isaiah 40:9, 41:8).

After the war was over, and George Washington became president of the United States of America, it seemed that disaster loomed on each horizon. One last time, Robert Morris appealed to Haym Salomon for aid. But this time Salomon was laying on his deathbed in his home in Philadelphia. Salomon could not refuse. Though dying of tuberculosis, he dragged his pain-racked body out of bed, left his home, went to the coffeehouse, and opened his brokerage operation one last time. Salomon had announcements printed and posted all over Philadelphia, announcing that the Haym Salomon brokerage would operate for a short time only. Investors streamed in to do business with Salomon. Haym was able to raise the money needed to save the new nation from disastrous bankruptcy.

Digging through the musty tomes of historical obscurity, we find such treasures as the following quotation: "The impression was abroad that Reb Hayyim [Mr. Haym] was a *nadib meod*, a great philanthropist and a man of wealth, and there is evidence of his generosity to some European supplicants. Salomon, who was no bluffer, admitted in a letter to John Strettel, a London merchant: 'My business is a broker, and chiefly in bills of exchange, and so very extensive that I am generally known to the mercantile part of North America.' As the chief broker for Morris, as an agent for the French army and navy, for the French diplomatic representative and consuls, for the Dutch and the Spanish, he was in truth no small fry."[20]

Salomon is buried in Philadelphia's Mikveh Israel Cemetery in an unmarked grave. This plaque is on a brick wall bordering the cemetery. It was placed there by his great-grandson William Salomon in 1917.

To the Memory of
HAYM SALOMON
A native of Lissa Poland
Known as a Patriot in the Cause of
THE AMERICAN REVOLUTION
He died in January 1785
aged forty-five years
and was interred in this Cemetery
The location of the grave
being now unknown
this Tablet has been erected
by his great-grandson
William Salomon of New York
September, 1917

CHAPTER SIX

"And Nehemiah, who was the governor,
Ezra the priest and scribe, and the
Levites who taught the people said to
all the people, 'This day is holy to the
LORD your God; do not mourn nor
weep.' For all the people wept, when
they heard the words of the Law."

NEHEMIAH 8:9

My quest for Haym Salomon was coming to an end. It was a cold, rainy day in Philadelphia as I walked toward Mikveh Israel Cemetery. In my chilled hand was the key loaned to me by the Jewish Historical Society. I pushed the key into the strong padlock that secured the iron-barred fence surrounding the graveyard. The rusty hasp came free, and I opened the heavy iron gate. I had come to see the grave of one of America's greatest patriots.

There in that little Jewish cemetery, I found the last ironic footnote to this story. For quite some time I looked, examining the inscription on every tombstone, but I sought in vain. No memorial could I find marking the final resting place of Haym Salomon. At last, glancing up to a wall on one side of Mikveh Cemetery, my eyes fell upon a plaque fastened to the wall. I read these words: "To the Memory of Haym Salomon...interred in this Cemetery. The location of the grave being now unknown..." Silently, silently, the man who did so much for his beloved America fades from the pages of history. Even his own people, the Jewish people, have forgotten exactly where he lies below the earth.

I must confess that my heart welled with gratitude to this forgotten man. Standing in the rain, I determined that I would do all that I could to revive his memory in the heart of America. I was flooded with emotions ranging from sorrow to joy. I confess that there were tears in my eyes, but an exultant joy in my heart.

Joy? Yes, for I remembered that in 1975 the United States Postal Department published a stamp honoring Haym Salomon. By wondrous coincidence, in that same year, the Israeli government published a stamp honoring Harry S. Truman, the president of the United States who was the first head of state to give recognition to the new nation of Israel, when that nation was born anew in the fires of war and struggle on May 14, 1948.

As I stood in that cemetery, these words went through my mind, "Rest in peace, Haym Salomon. Your sacrifice was not in vain—your dream has been fulfilled. Your beloved America has survived, and on the shores of the blue Mediterranean, the homeland you never saw, but only dreamed of, is in existence once again. An American president gave it first recognition, and in a hostile world, it is America that has been its sponsor and protector. May God grant that the dream remain a reality until the coming of Messiah and His Kingdom."

As pressure mounts on our nation to betray our Israeli allies, please take a moment to remember the debt we owe—a debt amounting to our very existence as a free nation. A free nation where the Church, for over 200 years, has found a safe haven. The United States of America is the only nation in history, since the founding of the Church, which has granted all of its citizens, in a pluralistic society, complete freedom of religion. How much we owe the forgotten Jew of Philadelphia, American patriot Haym Salomon!

Endnotes

1. Charles Spencer Hart, *George Washington's Son of Israel* (Freeport, NY: Books for Libraries Press, 1937), 5.

2. Reuben Fink, *America and Palestine* (New York: American Zionist Emergency Council, 1944), 18–19.

3. Jacob Rader Marcus, *Early American Jewry* (Philadelphia: Jewish Publication Society of America, 1953), 133.

4. Ibid., 135.

5. Ibid., 136.

6. Washington Irving, *The Life of George Washington*, vol. 1 (New York: Cooperative Publication Society, 1858), 263–265.

7. Shirley Milgrim, *Haym Salomon, Liberty's Son* (New York: Jewish Publication Society, 1979), 32.

8. *The New Encyclopaedia Britannica, Micropedia*, vol. 8 (Chicago: Encyclopaedia Britannica, 1981), 817.

9. Marcus, *Early American Jewry*, 145.

10. Milgrim, *Haym Salomon, Liberty's Son*, 79.

11. Ibid., 81–82.

12. Marcus, *Early American Jewry*, 141.

13. Hart, *George Washington's Son of Israel*, 5.

14. Ibid., 12.

15. Mortimer J. Adler, ed., *The Annals of America*, vol. 2 (Chicago: Encyclopaedia Britannica, 1976), 574.

16. Charles Edward Russell, *Haym Salomon and the Revolution* (Freeport, NY: Books for Libraries Press, 1930), 276–277.

17. John Clark Ridpath, *Ridpath's History of the World* (Cincinnati: Jones Brothers Publishing, 1911), 612.

18. Russell, *Haym Salomon and the Revolution*, 294.

19. Marcus, *Early American Jewry*, 134.

20. Ibid., 152.

Selected Bibliography

Adler, Mortimer J., ed. *The Annals of America*. 18 vols. Chicago: Encyclopaedia Britannica, 1976.

Ausubel, Nathan. *Pictorial History of the Jewish People*. New York: Crown Publishers, 1953.

Ben-Sasson, H. H., ed. *A History of the Jewish People*. Cambridge, MA: Harvard University Press, 1969.

Fast, Howard. *Haym Salomon, Son of Liberty*. New York: Julian Messner, 1941.

Fink, Reuben. *America and Palestine*. New York: American Zionist Emergency Council, 1944.

Friedman, Lee M. *Pilgrims in a New Land*. Westport, CT: Greenwood Press, 1948, reprint 1976.

Hart, Charles Spencer. *George Washington's Son of Israel*. Freeport, NY: Books for Libraries Press, 1937.

Hertzberg, Arthur. *The Jews in America*. New York: Simon and Schuster, 1989.

Irving, Washington. *The Life of George Washington*. New York: Cooperative Publication Society, 1858.

Knight, Vick, Jr. *Send for Haym Salomon*. Alhambra, CA: Borden Publishing, 1976.

Marcus, Jacob Rader. *Early American Jewry*. Philadelphia: Jewish Publication Society of America, 1953.

Milgrim, Shirley. *Haym Salomon, Liberty's Son*. New York: Jewish Publication Society, 1979.

New Encyclopaedia Britannica, Micropedia, The. Chicago: Encyclopaedia Britannica, 1981.

Rezneck, Samuel. *Unrecognized Patriots—The Jews in the American Revolution*. Westport, CT: Greenwood Press, 1975.

Ridpath, John Clark. *Ridpath's History of the World*. Cincinnati: Jones Brothers Publishing, 1911.

Russell, Charles Edward. *Haym Salomon and the Revolution*. Freeport, NY: Books for Libraries Press, 1930.

About the Author

DAVID ALLEN LEWIS is an ordained Assemblies of God clergyman and founder of Christians United for Israel. He has authored over 30 books, produced 39 television documentaries on location throughout Israel, and traveled to the Middle East 67 times, promoting the welfare of the Church, Israel, and the Jewish people.

He has conferred on numerous occasions with Israel's heads of government, including Prime Ministers Begin, Shamir, Netanyahu, and Sharon as well as members of Israel's parliament, mayors, and presidents. He has also established many relationships with moderate Palestinian leaders, US senators, congressmen, and ambassadors, as well as Jewish and Christian leaders. He has appeared as a witness on the Middle East before the Senate Foreign Relations Committee in Washington, DC.

Dr. Lewis received his biblical education at Central Bible College in Springfield, Missouri; a Doctor of Literature from Louisiana Baptist University and Theological Seminary in 1998; a Bachelor of Ministry and Master of Arts in Theology from Pacific International University in 2000; an Honorary Doctor of Divinity degree from the College and Seminary of St. Paul in Rome, Italy; and a doctoral degree from Pacific International University in 2001.

Dr. Lewis has spoken in churches, conferences, clergy seminars, colleges, camp meetings and taught courses in eschatology and apocalyptic literature on both secular and theological college campuses.

He and his wife Ramona have been married for over 50 years. They have two daughters, two grandchildren, and three great-grandchildren.

To order Dr. Lewis's books, a catalog, or product list, order online at www.davidallenlewis.com/store.htm or write to: David Lewis Ministries, P.O. Box 14444, Springfield, MO 65814.

Don't just read about
Bible prophecy–Be a part of it!

Your Israel Connection®

Bridges for Peace

in action

BRIDGES FOR PEACE

Bridges for Peace is a Jerusalem-based, Bible-believing Christian organization supporting Israel and building relationships between Christians and Jews worldwide through education and practical deeds expressing God's love and mercy.

It is our desire to see Christians and Jews working side by side for better understanding and a more secure Israel. Founded in 1976, Bridges for Peace seeks to be a ministry of hope and reconciliation. Through programs both in Israel and worldwide, we are giving Christians the opportunity to express actively their biblical responsibility before God to be faithful to Israel and the Jewish community. For too long, Christians have been silent. For too long, the Jewish community has had to fight its battles alone. It is time Christian individuals and congregations speak up for the people who gave us the Bible.

We are committed to the following goals:

❖ To encourage meaningful and supportive relationships between Christians and Jews in Israel and around the world.

❖ To educate and equip Christians to identify with Israel, the Jewish people, and the biblical/Hebraic foundations of our Christian faith.

❖ To bless Israel and the Jewish people in Israel and worldwide, through practical assistance, volunteer service, and prayer.

❖ To communicate Christian perspectives to the attention of Israeli leaders and the Jewish community-at-large.

❖ To counter anti-Semitism worldwide and support Israel's divine God-given right to exist in her God-given land.

When you come to Israel, we would like to meet you or speak to your group. Please contact us in advance to schedule a visit: intl.travel@bridgesforpeace.com (see addresses on next page).

We invite you to join us in blessing Israel by becoming an active bridge-builder and participating in fulfilling biblical prophecy through the vital and important work of Bridges for Peace.

Please use our coupon on page 55 and give Israel your support today!

Visit our Web site: www.bridgesforpeace.com

INTERNATIONAL

John Howson
National Director
CANADA

Atsumi Takada
National Director
JAPAN

Pam Thomas
National Director
UNITED KINGDOM

Rebecca Brimmer
International President
and CEO
JERUSALEM

Jim Solberg
National Director
UNITED STATES

Keith Buxton
National Director
AUSTRALIA

Chris Eden
National Director
SOUTH AFRICA

Brian Ashford
National Coordinator
NEW ZEALAND

Contact us for more information or help in planning activities in your area.

INTERNATIONAL HEADQUARTERS: P.O. Box 1093, Jerusalem, Israel
Tel: (972) 2-624-5004, FAX: (972) 2-624-6622, intl.office@bridgesforpeace.com

AUSTRALIA: P.O. Box 1785, Buderim, Queensland 4556
Tel: (61) 7-5453-7988, FAX: (61) 7-5476-5838, adminaust@bridgesforpeace.com.au

CANADA: P.O. Box 21001, RPO Charleswood, Winnipeg, MB R3R 3R2
Tel: (1) 204-489-3697, FAX: (1) 204-786-2051, bfp@mts.net

JAPAN: Taihei Sakura Bldg 5F, 4-13-2 Taihei, Sumida-Ku, Tokyo 130 0012
Tel: (81) 3-5637-5333, FAX: (81) 3-5637-5331, bfp@bfpj.net

NEW ZEALAND: P.O. Box 10142, Te Mai, Whangarei
Tel/FAX: (64) 9-434-6527, bfpnz@paradise.net.nz

SOUTH AFRICA: P.O. Box 1848, Durbanville 7551
Tel/FAX: (27) 21-975-1941, info@bridgesforpeace.co.za

UNITED KINGDOM: 63 Castle Street, Maesteg, Bridgend, Wales CF34 9YL
Tel: (44) 1656-739494, FAX: (44) 1656-733994, bfpuk@btconnect.com

UNITED STATES: PMB 33145, 5103 S. Sheridan Rd., Tulsa, OK 74145-7627
Tel: (1) 800-566-1998, FAX: (1) 321-541-1079, Product orders: (1) 888-669-8800
postmaster@bfpusa.org

Operation EZRA

Your Hands of Blessing in Israel

FOOD: Our food bank in Jerusalem—the largest of its kind in Israel—distributes food to needy immigrant and Israeli families and assists Jewish organizations serving the poor.

WELCOME PROGRAM: We welcome new immigrants to Israel with a large gift package that includes a kitchen set of pans and utensils, blankets, school kits for the children, and a 3-volume Hebrew-Russian (or 2-volume Hebrew-Spanish) edition of the Hebrew Scriptures.

CHEER BASKETS: A wrapped basket, filled with treats—such as cookies, candy, nuts, and tea—brings hope and encouragement to victims of terrorism, shut-ins, and the elderly who need a tangible expression of God's love.

ADOPTION: Sponsors adopt an Israeli individual or family for one year, providing food (fruits, vegetables, canned goods, dairy and paper products), bus tickets, and financial assistance for special needs and becoming personally connected by exchanging letters.

HOME REPAIR: Teams of skilled construction workers renovate homes of the poor and elderly in dire conditions, fixing leaky plumbing, replacing broken windows, painting, plastering, rewiring, and installing cabinets.

DENTAL: Because Israeli health insurance does not cover dental care, this fund pays for expensive dental visits, bringing smiles back to the faces of the poor who suffer from tooth pain.

GLEANING: This fund keeps our trucks on the road, transporting our volunteers to fields and factories all over Israel to collect tons of free food and products.

PROJECT RESCUE: Our financial assistance helps pay for the expense of passports, visas, ground transportation, and lodging for Jews in the countries of the Diaspora who want to emigrate to Israel.

PROJECT TIKVAH (HOPE): Soup kitchens provide hot, nutritious meals—often the only meal eaten in a day—for elderly and sick Jews who cannot emigrate to Israel, and heaters are purchased for the winter season for those living in unheated quarters.

VICTIMS OF WAR: We minister to anyone touched by terrorism, delivering special cheer baskets to the wounded in hospitals after a suicide bombing and to the bereaved. Special needs, such as wheelchairs, food vouchers, and financial assistance for medical bills are provided for those in long-term rehabilitation.

ADOPT AN ISRAELI TOWN: Currently, we are assisting 12 Israeli towns—from the Galilee to the Negev—that are experiencing severe economic hardship. Working through social workers and community officials, we give parcels of food for needy families, many of them new immigrants.

FEED A CHILD: Thousands of Israeli school children live below the poverty line and cannot afford to buy lunch, even at a subsidized cost. Your gift will provide hot lunches at school, birthday and holiday gifts, school books, a backpack filled with supplies, and funds for special needs during the summer.

Discipleship & EDUCATION

Sending forth the Word from Zion

PUBLICATIONS FROM JERUSALEM: Our *Dispatch from Jerusalem* is a 20-page, full-color, bimonthly publication featuring pertinent news and stories from Israel. Enjoy our *Israel Teaching Letter*, a monthly in-depth study shedding light on the fuller meanings of biblical concepts from the Hebraic roots of Scripture.

Subscribe to our *Israel Current News Update with Prayer Focus*, a weekly e-mail of news articles from Israel with prayer focuses and Scriptures.

WEB SITE: Visit www.bridgesforpeace.com to access our news updates, teaching letters, and *Dispatch* articles, view activities and tours sponsored by our eight national offices, sign up for our 24-Hour Prayer Chain, tune in to our Israel Mosaic Radio program, read about our volunteer program, make a donation, and much more.

ISRAEL MOSAIC RADIO: News, interviews, and teaching are broadcast from Jerusalem to radio stations around the world and are also available on our Web site.

RESOURCES: For books and other items to help you understand Israel, see "Resources" and "Shopping" on our Web site or check with your national office.

BRIDGE-BUILDING ACTIVITIES: SOLIDARITY MISSION: Our annual seminar in Jerusalem promotes better Christian–Jewish relationships.

STUDY TOURS: A visit to Israel—from the northern Galilee to the southern Negev—brings the Bible to life as never before.

CHRISTIAN LEADERS FORUMS: One-day seminars about Israel especially designed for pastors and Christian leaders.

LAND OF THE BIBLE EXPERIENCE: A developing educational center where biblical themes are taught through drama and interactivity, biblical models, a bookstore, and a gift shop.

ZEALOUS8:2: This branch of Bridges for Peace aims at reaching and impacting the young adult generation (18–30) with the message of God's plan and purpose for the nation of Israel.

VOLUNTEERING: People of all ages from all over the world come to Jerusalem to help us bless God's people in Israel. We need your skills and talents for short- or long-term service! Click on "Volunteering" on our Web site.

51

BRIDGES FOR PEACE

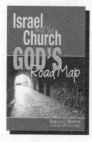

Israel and the Church: God's Road Map
Rebecca J. Brimmer and Bridges for Peace Leaders

The world has made a plan for the Middle East, but they have forgotten God's Road Map. Discover God's plans and participate with Him in this end-time drama. This anthology covers topics such as the feasts, *aliyah* (immigration to Israel), Israel in prophecy, anti-Semitism, Jerusalem, and Replacement Theology.
US $15.00 + S&H (256 pages)

"For Zion's Sake I Will Not Be Silent"
Scripture Guide to Praying for Israel

Rebecca J. Brimmer

This Scripture guide organizes many Scripture passages relating to Israel into specific categories. Now, you can learn the scriptural promises God has given concerning Israel and can pray effectively using your Bible as your guide.
US $13.00 + S&H (107 pages)

The Children of Abraham
An Exploration of Our Biblical Heritage
Cheryl Hauer

Teach the deep roots of our Christian faith and our connection to the Jewish people! This 24-unit curriculum includes chapter lesson plans, resource sections, eight full-color Judaica teaching cards, and a two-hour teachers' video. An ideal curriculum for Sunday school, VBS, Christian day schools, homeschooling, and more.
US $99.95 + S&H

Disengagement Through the Lens
A Glimpse at Gush Katif Before and After
William King & Emilia Kahan

Full-color photos, firsthand accounts, and historical insights tell the story of Gush Katif and northern Samaria, the 25 Jewish communities that were uprooted and destroyed by Israeli Prime Minister Ariel Sharon's Disengagement Plan in August 2005.
US $17.00 + S&H (103 pages)

52

BOOKSTORE

Forgotten Patriot
The Story of Haym Salomon

David Allen Lewis

Many Jews fought in the Revolutionary Army, and many contributed financially to the cause, but none did as much as Haym Salomon—a forgotten hero in American history. He gave everything to help establish the United States.

US $5.00 + S&H (64 pages)

Enter His Gates
To Your Jewish Roots

Susan Marcus

A quick-reference guide to understanding our Jewish roots. This book explains the source, function, and importance of the mezuzah, prayer shawl, Shabbat, blessings, etc. It even provides blessings in Hebrew and recipes for the feasts. Beautifully illustrated in full color.

US $20.00 + S&H (94 pages)

Listening to the Language of the Bible
Hearing It Through Jesus' Ears

Lois Tverberg with Bruce Okkema

Sometimes Scripture's Hebraic ideas and imagery sound foreign to our ears. When we enter the minds of its ancient authors and attempt to understand the culture, place, and time in which they were living, we discover new depths and meaning.

US $9.95 + S&H (174 pages)

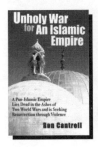

Unholy War for An Islamic Empire

Ron Cantrell

Islamist terror has moved outside the Middle East. What do we need to know? How should we live in light of today's pressures?

US $14.95 + S&H (220 pages)

Sounds of Zion

An exciting music video of 12 moving songs by Christian artists. Filmed on location in Israel, you will rejoice with those who bring God's message in music from Jerusalem, the city of the Great King.

US $14.95 + S&H

Are You Planning to Visit Israel?
You Can Be a Blessing!

If you are planning a trip, you can bring personal items for distribution in our Operation Ezra programs. Simply purchase these items yourself (or with help from your church or prayer group) and pack them into your suitcase (or extra suitcase, which is allowed for those coming from North America). There are no customs duties on these items. If your group brings 10 or more suitcases for Bridges for Peace, we will meet you at the airport. We can pick up fewer suitcases in Jerusalem at your hotel. Prior arrangements for these services must be made with your national office.

What is needed?

- New items for newborns
- New children's clothing of all kinds (to age 12)
- New underwear, shoes, socks, and sweaters
- School supplies for children
- New toys (nonverbal)
- Small kitchen utensils and gadgets
- New kitchen and bathroom towels and pot holders
- Flat sheets (not fitted)
- New medical supplies, e.g., surgical tape, gauze, bandages
- Toothpaste, toothbrushes, soap, deodorant, and shampoo
- For women: hairbrushes, lipsticks, small purses, nail polish, eye makeup, scarves, earrings
- For men: shaving kits, wallets, belts
- For girls: hair items, sticker books, stickers, scarves, small photo albums, soft toys
- For boys: Superballs, stickers, sticker books, model cars, picture books
- For babies: baby shampoo, lotion, baby spoons, baby booties, diapers, soft toys, blankets

  PLEASE do not send vitamins or food. Israeli laws prohibit us from giving out these items.

Coordinate details with your national office. www.bridgesforpeace.com

Yes!

I want to bless Israel!

PROJECTS

- [ ] $_____ New Outreach Facility
- [ ] $_____ Adoption Program
  $50/month (one-yr. commitment)
- [ ] $_____ Feed a Child
  $50/month (one-yr. commitment)
- [ ] $_____ Adopt an Israeli Town
  $100/month (one-yr. commitment)
- [ ] $_____ Food (any size)
  $_____ Monthly
- [ ] $_____ Cheer Basket—$18
- [ ] $_____ Kitchen Gift—$50
- [ ] $_____ Blanket—$18
- [ ] $_____ Bible—$40 (3 volumes)
- [ ] $_____ School Kit—$5
- [ ] $_____ Home Repair
- [ ] $_____ Project Rescue—$300
- [ ] $_____ Project Tikvah—$30
- [ ] $_____ Victims of War
- [ ] Dental Program
  $_____ $35 per individual
  $_____ $70 per couple
  $_____ $140 per family
- [ ] $_____ Gleaning—$5 or more
- [ ] $_____ Education
- [ ] $_____ Leaders Forum—$60
- [ ] $_____ Israel Mosaic Radio
- [ ] $_____ Land of the Bible
  Experience
- [ ] $_____ Zealous8:2
- [ ] $_____ Zealous8:2 Scholarship

BOOKS

- [ ] $_____ Israel and the Church: God's Road Map—$15
- [ ] $_____ Forgotten Patriot—The Story of Haym Salomon—$5.00
- [ ] $_____ "For Zion's Sake I Will Not Be Silent"—$13
- [ ] $_____ Enter His Gates—$20
- [ ] $_____ Unholy War for an Islamic Empire—$14.95
- [ ] $_____ The Children of Abraham (Curriculum)—$99.95
- [ ] $_____ Listening to the Language of the Bible—$9.95
- [ ] $_____ Disengagement Through the Lens—$17
- [ ] $_____ Sounds of Zion Video—$14.95

Total $ _____   *Please note that all prices are in US dollars.*

Shipping
Please figure your shipping charges according to the following:
Orders under US $20.00 add US $3.95
US $20.01 to US $50.00 add US $5.50
US $50.01 to US $100.00 add 10%
US $100.00 and up add 8%

Payment Options

- [ ] Check
- [ ] VISA
- [ ] Mastercard _____
- [ ] Discover

Credit Card #_____

Expires _____ / _____

Signature_____

Contact Information

Name_____

Address_____

City_____   State/Prov._____

Code_____   Country_____

Tel. (_____)_____   E-mail_____

55